Fearless

PERLA TAMEZ

BOOK SERIES BY FIG FACTOR MEDIA

WordPower Book Series

© Copyright 2021, Fig Factor Media, LLC.
All rights reserved.

All rights reserved. No portion of this book may be reproduced by mechanical, photographic or electronic process, nor may it be stored in a retrieval system, transmitted in any form or otherwise be copied for public use or private use without written permission of the copyright owner.

It is sold with the understanding that the publisher and the individual authors are not engaged in the rendering of psychological, legal, accounting or other professional advice. The content and views in each chapter are the sole expression and opinion of its author and not necessarily the views of Fig Factor Media, LLC.

For more information, contact:

Fig Factor Media, LLC | www.figfactormedia.com

Cover Design & Layout by Juan Pablo Ruiz
Printed in the United States of America

**ISBN: 978-1-957058-10-8
Library of Congress Control Number: 2021923569**

DEDICATION

To my father and mother, because through their grit, tenacity, and resilience, they taught me how to be fearless.

ACKNOWLEDGMENTS

I want to acknowledge my daughter's endurance. She proves that courage doesn't have an age requirement. If a nine-year-old can be fearless, so can you!

INTRO

In life, dreams beckon us on the banks beside our fears. This is why we need a loving relationship with our fear.

This is an ironic relationship because we're taught that fear is a danger zone. We're told fear is a red light that means: Stay away! Back off! But I can tell you: fearless is the opposite. To be fearless is to get close to fear, to inspect it, to dive in, to study it.

You have to take the wheel, reach for that school, travel worldwide, start that new company! We may not want to love our fear, but this is how we learn. This is how we grow. This is where the secrets of life are held. This is how we achieve our dreams.

It's time to leap in! Let's be fearless!

BORN FEARLESS

From the minute we're born, we are fearless. We have to be. We come into this world knowing nothing and we need to learn everything from scratch. Everything is new. We learn to speak, to walk, to love. We fall, but we pick ourselves up. This is part of our education. We need to know what we don't know. This puts us in a fearless position.

As adults, our decisions seem to hold more pressure. What if we fail? What if we make the wrong decisions? This is where fear comes in. But kids show us we have been fearless all along! We have been leaping into our fear since we leaped into life!

PANDORA'S BOX

Fear is a Pandora's Box with jewels inside. Inside every fear you open up, there is hope waiting to be released. This is the perspective we have to adopt. If you remain stuck in your doubt, you run away, you assume the worst—*El miedo te congela!*

But fear is good. If it's uncomfortable, dig into it! Calculate the risk. Know real threats (like an oncoming train) are different from your fears, projections, and uncertainty about the future. You can't see all the outcomes, so take that bold step anyway. You will find a beautiful Pandora's Box inside your unlocked fears, in the fears you learn to love!

FEAR AS EDUCATION

If you understand that fear is your education, your brain unlocks. This means that anything that brings you fear can also bring you the best life lessons. I have been able to conquer when I am fearless. I have had success through loving fear. Know that pushing through fear brings stretched and strengthened perspective, skills, knowledge. This creates a whole repertoire you didn't know you had! Often, the best lessons are self-taught, built on the foundation of your abilities, risks, and failures.

THE FEARLESS

The Fearless are as adaptable as chameleons and curious as cats. Adaptability keeps them supple and keeps their minds ready for whatever may come next. Curiosity lets them build their dreams! Fearless people are also willing to lose sometimes. If you lose, you learn. There is always a lesson in failure and pushing through this fear brings you closer to a win!

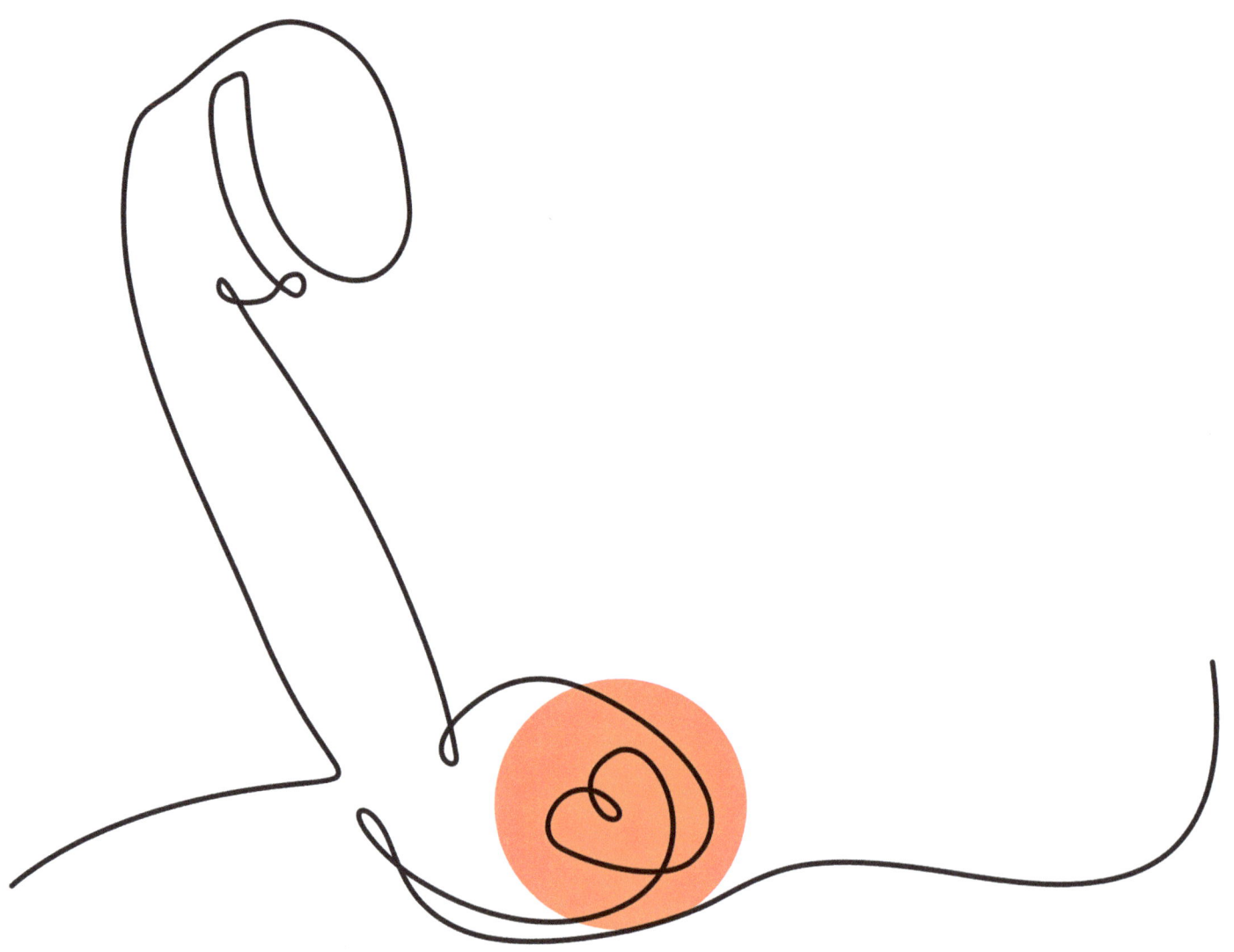

A FEARLESS ENTREPRENEUR

You can't wait for the right time to be brave. Being fearless helps you become who you are meant to be.

When I was 21 and started my first company, I was fearless. I opened up my company from the ground-up. My telephone line was connected to my bedroom in my parents' house! I didn't need an office to start, I didn't need to doubt, and I didn't need to judge myself harshly. I was fearless, ready to learn.

Start now! How can you be brave today? What fear do you need to love first?

ANECDOTE: AFRICA

Six years ago, I was visiting Ghana and had a three-hour drive to catch my flight home. When my driver and I stopped for food, he didn't eat. Why? He explained, "My three-year-old son has never tasted chicken. I'm saving it for him." Moved, I asked, "Can we take some food to your family?"

Now, I only had $80 and was visiting a stranger's home in a foreign country, but I reasoned: What could happen? I had a plane ticket. Maybe I wouldn't eat on the plane. No big deal. What if I was kidnapped? Or raped? What if I got AIDS? Even in the worst-case scenario, I had a solution—I could take AIDS medication. The kidnappers could call my family. I would process my trauma.

Fearless, I brought chicken, chips, and cokes to my driver's family. And this visit was the most rewarding human experience of my life!

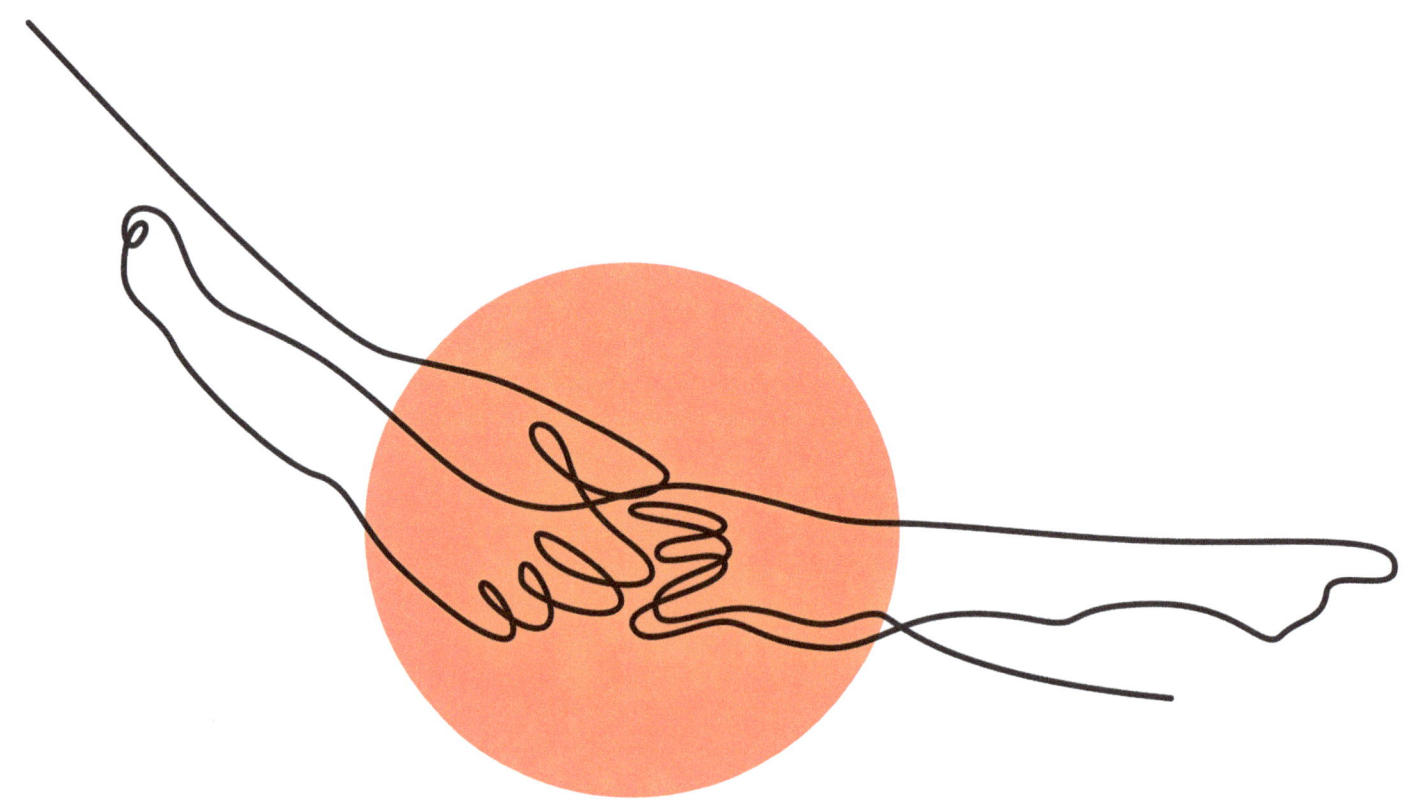

FEARLESS SERVICE

When we are fearless for ourselves and for our mission, we can be fearless for others.

When I joined Hispanic Star as a hub director, I recruited help leaders around the country for relief campaigns that brought people home essential goods. These leaders were super brave! Focused on the mission of helping others, they jumped into loving their fear. They were fearless in their service!

Are you being called to serve fearlessly?

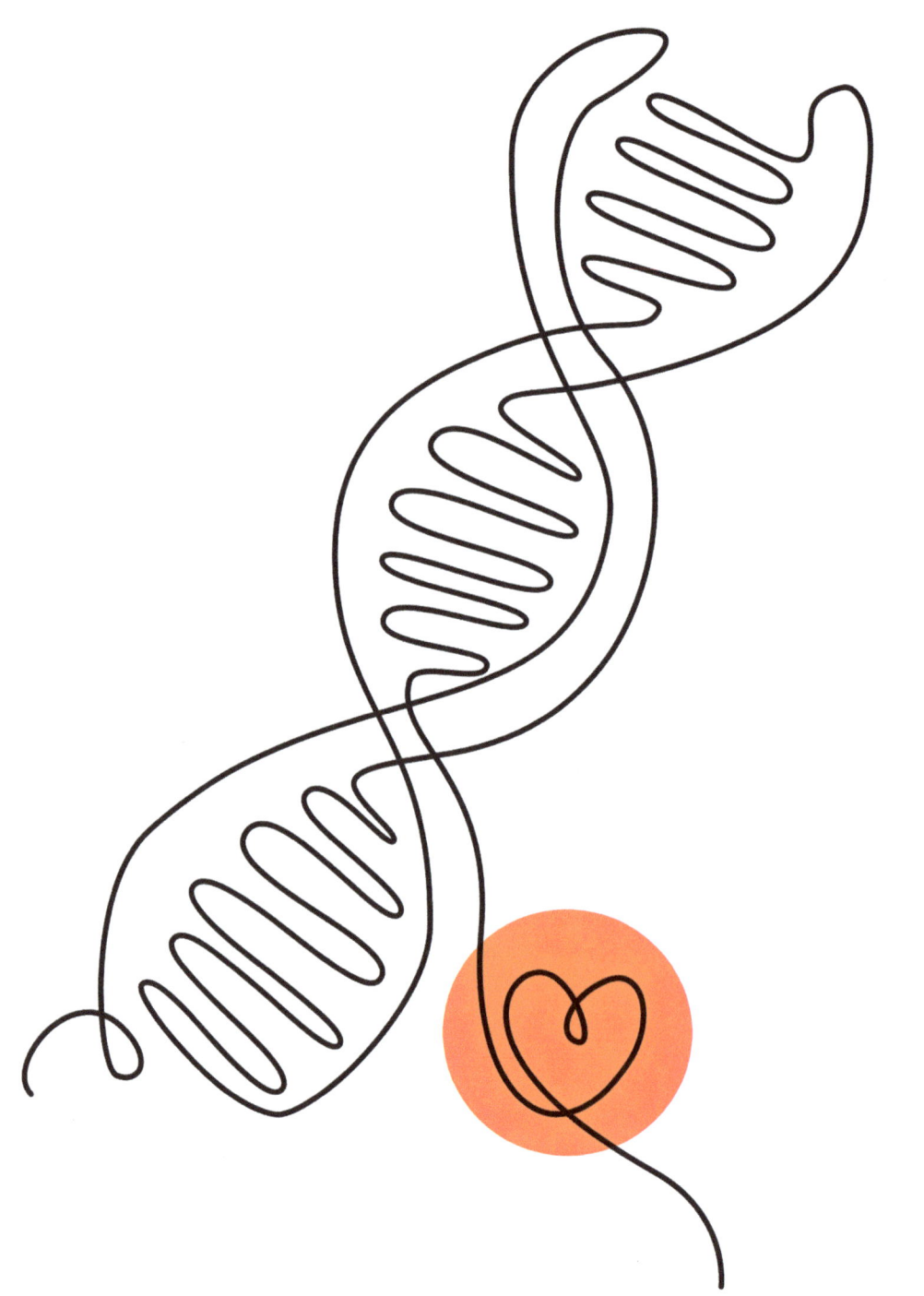

3 STEPS TO OVERCOME FEAR

I have a three-step process that I use to face my fears. It helps me move into fearlessness and take the bold path. This three-step model is a habit. With practice, you'll do it in milliseconds. And with it, you can dare yourself into fearlessness!

This practice is important because we have to be fearless 24/7! Life changes in a heartbeat. Bravery has to be part of our DNA, has to be like the blood in your veins. Fearlessness has to be a switch that's always activated. This three-step process can help…

1. ACKNOWLEDGE

The first step is to acknowledge the fear and name it. Are you afraid of taking a job in a new country? Are you afraid of what people will think if you start your business? Do you think taking a risk will lead to failure? Name it! When you name your fear, you accept it for what it is. Then you are ready to unpack it.

2. CATASTROPHIZE: WHAT'S THE WORST THAT COULD HAPPEN?

With your fear, imagine the worst possible thing that could happen. Often this is connected to failure, loss, or embarrassment. Are you afraid you'll be cut off from your friends in a new place? Are you worried you won't know how to solve new problems? Could something you built need to be completely redone?

Strong fears jump into our minds and collect our worry. But we don't stop the fear here.

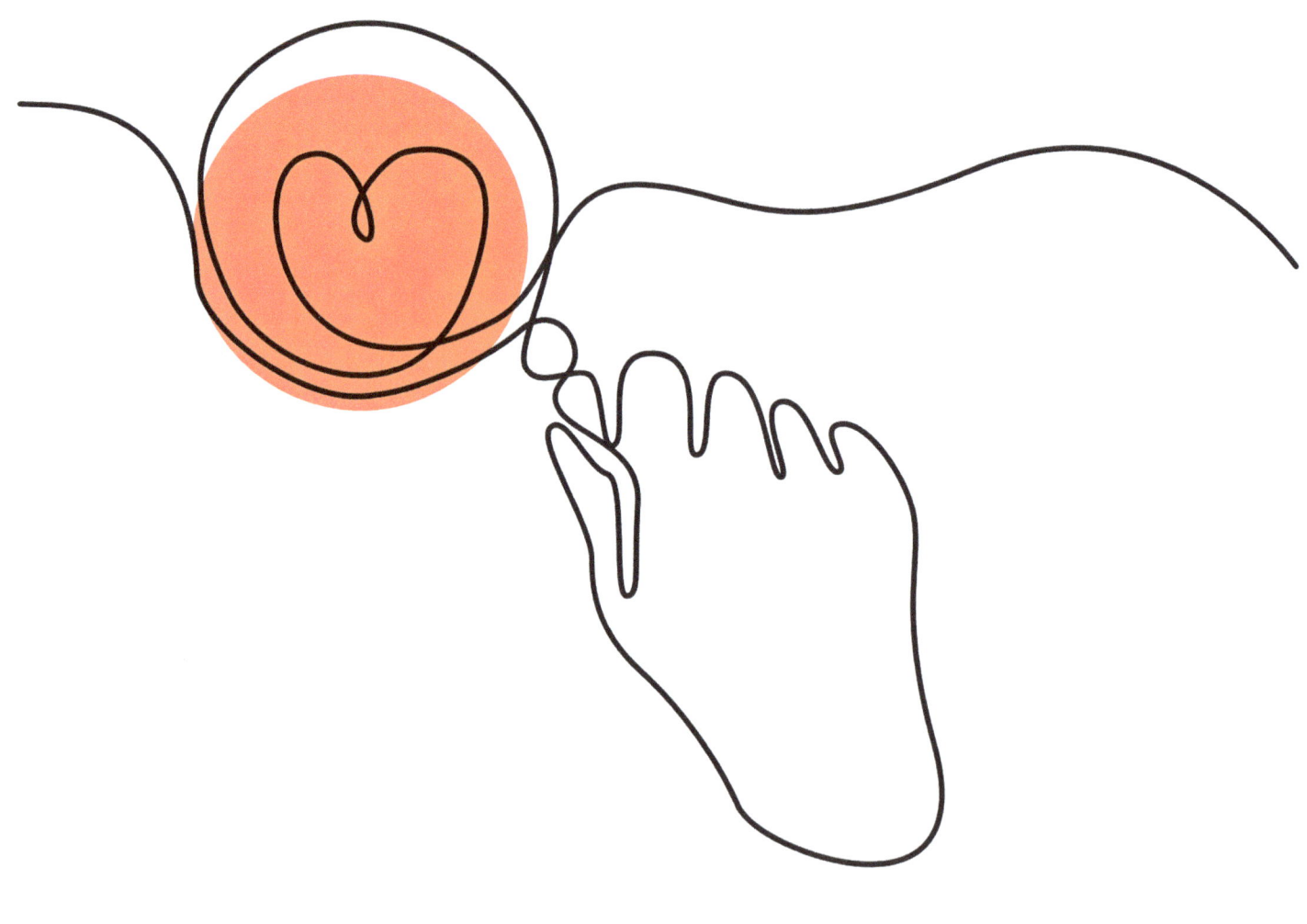

3. SOLVE

Now that you've thought of the worst that could happen, how would you solve this? Are there resources you can draw on, ways that you can steel yourself to face the problem if it was the absolute worst it could be? When you reflect on the worst and come up with a plan, you combat your fear. Once you solve the fearful outcome, you'll be able to void and veto your fear's strength and move into fearlessness.

THE CALL

This is the call: keep learning through your fear! When we master the abilities of our bodies, minds, and souls, we move, we innovate, we create. Once you dig into what held you back, you'll exploit your talents and passions. At that point you're invincible. Love your fear! Brave the world! Be fearless!

ABOUT THE AUTHOR

Perla Elizabeth Tamez is a visionary serial entrepreneur and licensed speech language pathologist assistant. She is an advocate for being fearless—and she shares her story with others to empower and unlock potential! Perla is also an advocate for healthcare and children's rights policies.

From childhood, Perla learned to run fiercely in the direction of her dreams. At 21, she founded her first outpatient pediatric clinic. Now, after creating 19 companies in 11 different industries, Perla has generated more than 9 digits of revenue in her businesses.
  Perla combines her passion for business and philanthropy in her pediatric clinics and in her advocacy for children's rights and health policies. This led her to join The Hispanic Star in 2020 as the Hub Director of the community operations centers, a team of American leaders who have impacted more than 400,000 families and distributed more than $ 7 million in household products.

To support organizations through education and strategic planning, Perla also founded the Love Soldiers Foundation with the mission of contributing to the well-being and quality of life of their communities.

www.ingramcontent.com/pod-product-compliance
Lightning Source LLC
Chambersburg PA
CBHW040021300426
43673CB00107B/342